W9-BEY-560

WITHDRAWN

PLYMOUTH PUBLIC LIBRARY
PLYMOUTH IN 46563

The World According to Martha

The World According to Martha

to Martha

Edited by Bill Adler

PLYMOUTH PUBLIC LIBRARY
PLYMOUTH IN 46563

McGraw-Hill

New York   Chicago   San Francisco   Lisbon   London   Madrid   Mexico City   Milan   New Delhi   San Juan
Seoul   Singapore   Sydney   Toronto

The
McGraw·Hill
Companies

Copyright © 2006 by Bill Adler Books, Inc. All rights reserved. Printed in the United States of America. Except as permitted under the United States Copyright Act of 1976, no part of this publication may be reproduced or distributed in any form or by any means, or stored in a data base or retrieval system, without the prior written permission of the publisher.

2 3 4 5 6 7 8 9 0   DOC/DOC   0 9 8 7 6 5

ISBN 0-07-146456-5

McGraw-Hill books are available at special quantity discounts to use as premiums and sales promotions, or for use in corporate training programs. For more information, please write to the Director of Special Sales, Professional Publishing, McGraw-Hill, Two Penn Plaza, New York, NY 10121-2298. Or contact your local bookstore.

 This book is printed on recycled, acid-free paper containing a minimum of 50% recycled, de-inked fiber.

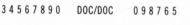

All images © Getty Images unless otherwise noted.

contents

introduction

Martha Stewart has the look and manner of a woman born into wealth and brought up in the plenty and luxury of a prosperous household. The real Martha Stewart, however, was born Martha Helen Kostyra in Jersey City, New Jersey, on August 2, 1941. Her mother was a school teacher, and her father was a pharmaceutical salesman whose strong work ethic and perfectionism formed the backbone of his daughter's drive to succeed.

Martha Kostyra began her transformation into the Martha Stewart we know when she married Andrew Stewart, took his name, and stepped into the Manhattan upper-class household and lifestyle of the Stewart family. With her keen powers of observation and innate good taste, combined with a strong desire to better herself and a true business acumen, Martha Kostyra transformed herself into Martha Stewart, progressing from tastemaker to celebrity to icon to brand. Like Oprah and Cher, Martha Stewart is such a singular individual that she needs to be called only by her first name. Everyone knows who "Martha" is. Or thinks he or she does.

It was in her early life in Nutley, New Jersey, in a house her parents and five brothers and sisters moved into when she was three, that Martha learned to take advantage of good fortune when it presented itself. The family was far from rich, but Martha's mother was clever and skillful as a homemaker, saving money by sewing most of the family's clothes. From her, Martha learned how to sew and knit, as well as how to prepare food, bake, cook, can vegetables, and preserve fruit—skills that would later shape her life's work.

From her father, Martha learned how to garden and take care of plants, shrubs, and vegetables. They often worked together in the garden, and Martha always tried as hard as she could to please her father by meeting, and even exceeding, his exacting standards. "I remember the first day that I was put out there on the garden path," Martha recalls. "We had this cobblestone path in our garden and it had weeds in it. And he said, 'Take out all the grass.' I think I was three. So I sat out there all day, you know, and I became his pet because of that."

Even when she was young, those around her could sense her drive for perfection and her pride in accomplishment—characteristics that would become her hallmarks. Martha did well in high school, earning a partial scholarship to Barnard College, where she majored in chemistry but later changed her areas of concentration to the history of art and architecture and European history. With her blonde hair and even features, she took on modeling jobs to earn money, eventually landing several magazine and TV spots, including ads for hair products from Clairol and Breck and for Tareyton cigarettes. Modeling taught Martha how to dress fashionably and present a poised demeanor, skills that would serve her well as she moved forward into the business world.

In a wedding dress that she and her mother made together, Martha married law student Andrew Stewart in 1961, when she was still a sophomore in college. When their daughter, Alexis, was born in 1964, they decided to leave their one-bedroom Manhattan apartment for a one-room former schoolhouse in Connecticut. The young couple set about renovating the property, which had no central heating or indoor plumbing. Martha would learn how to renovate and decorate hands-on from the ground up.

In 1967, Martha returned to the workforce, this time as a stockbroker on Wall Street, aided by her father-in-law, who also was a stockbroker. Successes followed not only because of her drive and attention to detail but also because she was one of a handful of women in the profession. Martha made sure that she was noticed by playing up her good looks and figure. "When I was a stockbroker, I was outrageous," she remembers. "I wore hot pants. I was one of the few women on Wall Street. I thought the way of dressing there was just stupid. I had beautiful long legs. I wore brown velvet hot pants with brown stockings and high heels."

Even with her accomplishments, however, working on Wall Street was intense and took away from the hours she could spend with her daughter, with her husband, and with other aspects of life on the home front. A laggard stock market helped seal her decision to leave Wall Street for the role of a suburban homemaker. But she took along the lessons she learned as a stockbroker. "I left Wall Street," she later remarked, "which was an extremely aggressive workplace and an extremely high-pressured place, to go home and to try to spend time with my daughter, fix up the house, paint the shutters and lay out the gardens, and it worked very well. I saw the value of that and turned it into a business."

This was the beginning of Martha Stewart, the domestic diva. She practiced her trade at a new house named Turkey Hill, which the couple bought in Westport, Connecticut, and which she still owns. Restoring the house to her specifications allowed Martha to hone her skills and apply an efficient, businesslike attitude to the tasks of home decorating. Martha and Andrew also worked in the garden, landscaping, planting fruit trees, pruning shrubs, and growing vegetables. It was clear to both of them that not only did Martha excel at this kind of work, but it also resonated deep within her. All her childhood time spent learning home skills from her father and mother was being put to use—and soon would begin to pay off.

While she and Andrew were renovating the house, Martha decided to try her hand at catering and placed ads in the local newspaper. Her first job was a wedding, and then, through word of mouth, her business flourished. Her big break came when a party she catered for her husband's publishing firm led to a book contract. *Entertaining,* published in 1982, was more than a cookbook. Along with recipes, more than 450 photographs invoked a genteel country lifestyle, an elegant yet back-to-basics way of living that struck a chord with overworked, stressed-out homemakers who saw in Martha a life they could dream about and try to achieve.

Although some food critics panned the recipes because they weren't able to duplicate them successfully, the book became a bestseller, propelling Martha into a new career as a domestic doyenne and arbiter of good taste and style. Other cookbooks followed, as did appearances on television talk shows and her own television specials. She was a regular contributor to *Family Circle* and wrote articles and columns for newspapers and other magazines.

Her growing stature both as a personality and as an expert on everything related to the home led to a consulting relationship with Kmart in 1987, but her early attempts at merging the discount retailer with the Martha Stewart style didn't take. She blamed it on Kmart's "ineffectual and unimaginative" upper management and severed the partnership. Neither side knew it at the time, but the relationship would be renewed a decade later, and it would make retailing history.

In 1990, Martha published the first issue of her magazine, *Martha Stewart Living.* It was an instant success. Its beautiful photographs of serenely decorated rooms (often rooms in her own home), stories about how to perform basic household tasks with style and efficiency, detailed instructions for craft projects, and sophisticated recipes appealed to a wide variety of American women. "There was nothing like it," Martha said later about her magazine. "It gave how-to information and beautifully photographed stories. The magazine has become very valuable to all demographics, from farmers to waitresses to college students."

With the magazine's circulation topping two million and her omnipresence across the media—television, books, and magazines—Martha had become an easy and fun target for ridicule. A raft of parodies emerged, ranging from *Saturday Night Live* sketches to spoof magazines such as *Is Martha Stewart Living?* She was skewered for her obsessive attention to detail and her relentless ambition. It was clear to anyone watching that Martha—now recognizable by her first name alone—would stop at nothing in her pursuit of perfection.

Despite her public image as a supremely confident homemaker and wife, Martha's personal life was less than perfect. In 1990, on the same day that her blockbuster book, *Weddings,* was published, her husband of 29 years filed for divorce, accusing her of mental cruelty. That streak of perfectionism that was so obvious to the public was just as apparent in her relationship with Andrew Stewart. "It's still a total mystery to me," Martha would later say. "I loved my husband. I noticed him growing away, but I didn't pay any attention to it. He said I was too much for him, that I was going too far too fast. What does that mean? If I should be punished for being too critical or too perfectionist, I've been punished."

However, the private Martha pushed the messy situation to one side and got on with her business as Martha Stewart—icon of all good things. In 1993 she launched her own syndicated television show and began to grow herself as a "brand" for a lifestyle of simplicity and taste. To control her brand, Martha created her own media empire by buying the rights to her magazine from Time Warner and taking the company—which now encompassed magazines with millions in circulation, newspaper columns, syndicated television programs, books, radio shows, Web sites, "Martha by Mail" catalogs, and her housewares marketed through Kmart—public in 1999. In typical Martha fashion, she brought a plate of homemade brioches to share with other members of the New York Stock Exchange on the company's first day of trading.

Not only did Martha's fans love her, but so did investors, who bid up the price of the Martha Stewart Living Omnimedia stock from $18 to a high of $52, ending at $36 on opening day. On paper, Martha was worth more than $1 billion. Few women, with the exception of Oprah Winfrey, had built a modern financial empire of this scope from scratch. Adding to her list of accomplishments, Martha was now a major economic force.

Her deal with Kmart was a brilliant move on her part. The retailer sells about a billion dollars worth of her signature products annually—ranging from cookware to garden supplies—although many observers predicted that she would fail. What they saw as a mismatch between an upscale Martha and a downscale retailer, Martha saw as an opportunity to make money by elevating the level of taste in America to her own high standards. Upscale or downscale, consumers wanted quality and style at a low price. Martha was savvy and talented enough to give it to them.

Just when it seemed as if nothing Martha did could go wrong, a bad decision on a busy day in December of 2001 would bring her down. Her sale of 4,000 shares of drugmaker ImClone the day before the stock plunged on news that the Food and Drug Administration (FDA) would not review the company's application for its cancer drug Erbitux helped her avoid a loss of $46,000—but it raised suspicions. Soon enough the public found out that the Securities and Exchange Commission was investigating allegations that she received insider information from her friend and ImClone founder Sam Waksal about the FDA's bad news.

Because of the scandal, Martha resigned from her position on the board of the New York Stock Exchange. In June 2003 a federal grand jury indicted Martha and her former broker on charges including securities fraud, obstruction of justice, and conspiracy. She was never indicted on insider trading but rather on the cover-up that followed. Now she was compelled to resign as chairwoman and CEO of her own company.

Martha protested her innocence, even taking out a full page ad in *USA Today* saying, "I want you to know that I am innocent—and that I will fight to clear my name."

She also had to fight for the integrity of Martha, the brand. CBS dropped her appearances on the *Early Show*. The price of Martha Stewart

Living Omnimedia plummeted, hitting a low of about $5 a share in late 2002. Although the most serious charge against her, fraud, was thrown out, Martha was tried and found guilty on March 5, 2004, on charges of conspiracy, obstruction of justice, and making false statements. Ironically, by some accounts, it was Martha's eye for detail that did her in. The jury could not believe that she had forgotten conversations and agreements made with her broker that contradicted the official documentation and other testimonies. Martha did not take the stand in her defense.

Instead of drawing out the appeals process—and the potential for continued erosion of the brand—Martha decided to render herself for six months at the federal prison camp in Alderson, West Virginia. Although very little so far has been revealed about her day-to-day life in prison, Martha apparently got along well with fellow inmates and was a model prisoner, even teaching a daily yoga class. She left jail on March 4, 2005, and immediately began to rebuild her empire and reconnect with her millions of supporters and fans.

Can she do it? Few are betting against Martha. Within days of leaving prison, she signed on for a new television series from Mark Burnett, the producer of *Survivor* and *The Apprentice*. She also penned a deal for a show on the Sirius satellite radio network. To her loyal fans and colleagues,

Martha made this promise on her release: "Our passion is, and always should be, to make life better."

There are those who admire Martha Stewart for the way she has elevated housekeeping from drudgery to a domestic art. There are also those who see in her an unpleasant combination of hint-giver Heloise and ruthless warrior Attila the Hun. But what both groups would agree on is that Martha Stewart is a force that cannot be ignored.

Here, then, from success, to failure, to rebirth is this remarkable woman's story in her own words.

on herself

"I don't sleep much. It's just not that interesting to me."

—*Post-Standard* (Syracuse, New York), March 24, 2000

"All I do is write cookbooks and teach people how to do good things."

—*New York Times* (New York, New York), November 24, 1996

"I struck a chord with women who were realizing that they better create a little balance in their existence. What I do helps them create that balance even if they never make a wreath."

—*Atlanta Journal-Constitution* (Atlanta, Georgia), January 26, 1996

"I try not to get jet-lagged—I don't have time to get jet-lagged."

—*People*, March 2, 1998

"Because you can. That's my new motto. Technology makes it possible, so it's going to get done."

—On why one should do as much as she does, *Forbes*, February 24, 1997

"The best part [of being Martha] is learning. I like learning and seeing."

—*Calgary Sun* (Calgary, Alberta, Canada), October 23, 1998

"It is kind of fun being without [electric] power—it makes you think. We have power outages [at her home in Westport, Connecticut] all the time."

—*Calgary Sun* (Calgary, Alberta, Canada), October 22, 1998

"I sighed a little sigh of relief that finally someone, maybe in a kind of overreaction, was taking me a little seriously. Because I fancy myself closer to that kind of study than to a parody."

—On being the object of study by popular culture academics,

Austin American-Statesman (Austin, Texas), August 7, 1998

"I am first and foremost a housewife with a home, with a garden, with everything that everybody wants."

—The Associated Press, August 1, 1998

"I live many different ways, and the Japanese style is one of my favorites."

—*Calgary Herald* (Calgary, Alberta, Canada), February 18, 1998

"I liked accomplishing a task very nicely. I liked getting all A's."

—*New York Times* (New York, New York), February 8, 1998

"I read two to four newspapers a day [because] I'm in a car three, four hours a day with Larry, who has been my driver for 18 years. We have a pact. We don't get out of the car till the [crossword] puzzle is done. Tuesday's was a bitch. Excuse me!"

—*Ventura County Star* (Ventura, California), October 17, 2000

"Every day there is something more important to cry about than business. I can handle my business, but I can't handle famine in Ethiopia."

—*Atlanta Journal-Constitution* (Atlanta, Georgia), August 29, 2000

"Living is limitless. There is always another color of paint, another project, another plant."

—*Vancouver Province* (Vancouver, British Columbia, Canada), July 9, 2000

"My worry is to find time to do it all."

—*USA Today*, July 3, 2000

"No other woman has created this kind of business in such a short time, from scratch, from, you know, baking cookies in the basement—if you can find that person, let me know—who took a company public and in the first day made, you know, over $1 billion. I mean that's—that's really fun."

—*60 Minutes II*, CBS, June 20, 2000

"The reason I stopped knitting for a while is that I had knit my father— while I was in college—I knitted him the most complicated cashmere scarf. Beautiful—it took me one year on the finest needles, using the finest yarn, and he lost it the first time he wore it. It wasn't funny."

—*The Early Show*, CBS, February 29, 2000

"To many onlookers, what I have accomplished may appear easy, but it was all done with hard work, old-fashioned elbow grease and a certain amount of emotional pain and suffering."

—*Times Colonist* (Victoria, British Columbia, Canada), July 14, 2001

". . . there is nothing that I regret in the process, and the lessons learned and the experiences I have gained are worth writing about in detail."

—On writing her autobiography, *HFN*, June 25, 2001

"What I try to do every single day is learn. I learned that from Barnard. I am really grateful to the college."

—University Wire, March 30, 2001

"I want to be Betty Crocker, and Betty Crocker never existed. I would love that."

—On weaning her image away from the company so that it could stand on its own,
Herald Sun (Durham, North Carolina), March 28, 2001

"I like doing a lot of things. I like mastering a lot of things. I like seeing if I can do something."

—*Larry King Live*, CNN, February 2, 2001

"Wherever you go, if people are considerate, that's the really important thing. I find almost everyone considerate and nice and that's what I look for in a community."

—On Seal Harbor, Maine, where Martha owns a home,
Bangor Daily News (Bangor, Maine), January 16, 2001

"A lot of people don't see my sense of humor. Generally, I'm pretty straightforward on the television show because it's my teaching approach. But I have a very good sense of humor, [although] sometimes it's maybe too sophisticated for people. But I like poking fun at myself."

—*The Gazette* (Montreal, Quebec, Canada), April 1, 2002

"If I can make fun of a glass of water, it just makes viewers feel, 'She's OK.' They'll laugh, and they'll think: 'Don't take it all so seriously.' Do it when you can, do it when you have time, do it when you're in the mood."

—*Times Colonist* (Victoria, British Columbia, Canada), April 1, 2002

"I do what I please and I do it with ease."

—High school yearbook entry, cited by *People in the News*, *CNN*, May 4, 2002

"I don't know why people don't like me. I'm not perfect. The perception that I am perfect I think got kind of mixed up with the idea that what we're trying to teach is the best possible standard out there. So if I were going to make a cake, Barbara, my cake can't be a flop."

—*20/20* interview with Barbara Walters, cited by *Vancouver Sun*

(Vancouver, British Columbia, Canada), November 6, 2003

"I'm real lucky, because I am able to sort of compartmentalize. I can be concerned on one hand, and be productive on the other hand. . . . I can still sleep."

—*Ottawa Citizen* (Ottawa, Ontario, Canada), January 28, 2003

"You know, in China they say, 'The thinner the chopsticks, the higher the social status.' Of course, I got the thinnest I could find. That's why people hate me."

—*National Post* (Toronto, Ontario, Canada), January 27, 2003

"[As a] First Lady, [she was] knocked to death and now [she's a] senator. You know, a very important person, still. Because she's smart, she's worthy, she's great. You know, that's what I hope I'll be thought of as."

—On Hillary Clinton, The Associated Press, January 26, 2003

"I don't play great tennis. I'm not very good at carpentry. And I've never tried hang-gliding."

—On things she doesn't do well, *San Jose Mercury News*

(San Jose, California), April 15, 1995

"I consider myself one of the original feminists. I'm trying to help give women back a sense of pleasure and accomplishment in their homes."

—*Canberra Times* (Canberra, Australia), December 4, 1999

"I love going to the juice bars. I don't know about you, but I'm sort of like a fanatic at the juice bar."

—*CBS This Morning*, CBS, January 15, 1999

on fans

"If we get 10,000 questions [from fans] about knives, it means that we will make knives."

—*Capital Times* (Madison, Wisconsin), October 13, 2000

"I promise I'll think long and hard before I accept another invitation to your chilly and downright unfriendly city again."

—Letter to Buffalo newspaper after leaving a book signing without satisfying fans' requests for autographs, *The Record* (Bergen County, New Jersey), September 3, 1996 (This letter was sent a month earlier but printed just after Martha's next letter.)

"I am happy to be coming back. I didn't want to be banned in Buffalo."

—After smoothing over the rift with Buffalo fans, *Buffalo News* (Buffalo, New York), August 28, 1996

on her critics

"The flak comes from people who just don't get it. The people who get it are a lot more numerous than the people who don't get it."

—*Atlanta Journal-Constitution* (Atlanta, Georgia), January 26, 1996

"I could have done it better."

—On the parody magazine, *Is Martha Stewart Living?*, *Minneapolis Star Tribune*

(Minneapolis, Minnesota), November 21, 1996

"Utterly bad taste. They're taking what I do—well-researched, well-documented and beautifully presented—and minimizing its importance."

—On *National Lampoon's Rolling Your Own Condoms*, *Hamilton Spectator* (Hamilton,

Ontario, Canada), February 12, 1997

"No one has accused Julia Child of stealing the French bread recipe . . . from French bakers. I don't consciously go and plagiarize people's work. If I were more sensitive, my life could be ruined by all this. I have inured myself to this kind of criticism. I don't care anymore. But I do care that my readers like what I do."

—*USA Today*, December 18, 1989

"I don't think they're funny enough. I would do them myself. But I don't have the time."

—On parodies of her magazine, *Martha Stewart Living, USA Today*, December 8, 1999

"It probably just makes me more human."

—On being the butt of jokes, *BusinessWeek*, January 17, 2000

on customers

"It's a minute-to-minute task to keep up with technology and customer demands. It's a constant thing."

—*Contra Costa Times* (San Francisco, California), June 25, 2000

"I try to treat them [consumers] like my friend and a colleague, and it works if they feel involved."

—*Marketing News*, March 30, 1998

"Everything you see, except for me, . . . is for sale."

—After showing the audience at a Chicago trade show a slide of a kitchen with her in the center, *Chicago Sun-Times* (Chicago, Illinois), January 15, 2001

"What do they need and want? Those are our mantras."

—*Star Phoenix* (Saskatoon, Saskatchewan, Canada), June 6, 2002

"We found there was a serious need for products to help the consumer keep a certain design scheme. It's very challenging to make it work, and this collection helps you become an expert at pulling all the elements of a room together."

—*Tulsa World* (Tulsa, Oklahoma), May 18, 2003

"I listen and I listen. One of my best qualities is that I listen and I make judgments on what I hear. And I have done that since the beginning of this business. To me, the most important persons to listen to are my readers, my viewers, my listeners, and my Internet users. I read every letter. I think about what they say, and I try to respond to them in as favorable a way as possible."

—*Moneyline News Hour*, CNN, October 19, 1999

"It's really targeted to people who don't know a lot about style."

—On her Everyday line of home furnishings, The Canadian Press,

May 29, 1998

"This [Martha Stewart Living Omnimedia] will be one of the most important companies for the homemaker ever."

—*Advertising Age,* October 16, 2000

"My ideas are good. I know what women want."

—*Newsweek,* December 1, 1986

on being a perfectionist

"*I'm actually setting all my silverware out backward now. Dyslexic table settings, so some people don't get intimidated [by my perfectionist attitude].*"

—*Seattle Post-Intelligencer* (Seattle, Washington), August 26, 2000

"*I continue to be as picky and as impossible as ever. I am a perfectionist, and especially when you're doing the kind of thing that people are looking at and trying to learn from, it's terribly important to do it in the finest fashion possible.*"

—*Buffalo News* (Buffalo, New York), December 8, 1996

"So when they look at a chicken, they can look at the picture in the book, then look at the chicken and see if it is an example of perfection. . . . So guess what? You can do that in other parts of life, too."

—*Financial Times* (London, England), August 25, 2000

"I have proven that being a perfectionist can be profitable and admirable when creating content across the board: in television, books, newspapers, radio, video."

—*St. Petersburg Times* (St. Petersburg, Florida), August 27, 2000

"You can be a taskmaster, and you can uphold your standards. And you can create standards of perfection and quality."

—*The Commercial Appeal* (Memphis, Tennessee), August 24, 2000

"I think I'm demanding. I think that I am a perfectionist. I think that I'm fair. And I think that people who work for me and get along with me realize what a good result there is."

—*Larry King Live*, CNN, February 2, 2001

on entertaining

"When it comes to entertaining, the best room in the house isn't in the house. It's outside."

—*Adweek,* May 23, 1988

"I like short-order cooking at breakfast; you can get rid of your guests really early."

—Tongue-in-cheek remark about entertaining friends in the morning,
St. Louis Post-Dispatch (St. Louis, Missouri), November 11, 1998

"Personally, I love to create spooky environments to celebrate Halloween, and sound effects are a big part of the fun."

—From a CD entitled *Martha Stewart Living's*
Spooky Scary Sounds for Halloween,
cited by *The Record* (Kitchener-Waterloo,
Ontario, Canada), October 19, 2000

❧

"Since the objective of these dinners is to get to know people from Martha Stewart Living Omnimedia, guests will be chosen at random."

—E-mail to 65 staff members directing them to open their homes for dinner parties of 10 employees each, which would encompass the company's 600 staffers, *San Francisco Chronicle* (San Francisco, California), December 7, 2001

"The more ideas I have, the more creativity I can express, the more happy I am, and of course, the more happy the guests are."

—*Orange County Register* (Orange County, California), November 2, 1988

"Keep it simple. Focus on one great dish. Say, coq au vin. Buy the best bottle of wine you can afford. Do a salad. Maybe a seasonal fruit dessert from a bakery. Use big plates and napkins. That way, people don't need a table. They can balance the plate on the lap. Sitting on the floor is fine. Work with the limited space and limit the number of guests."

—*Chicago Tribune* (Chicago, Illinois), December 22, 1986

© Corbis/James Levnse

"The cocktail party is still my favorite way to entertain groups of friends, as well as one of my favorite catering assignments. Hors d'oeuvres, I have discovered, can be almost any type of food, of any ethnic origin. I love hors d'oeuvres because they provide an opportunity to be wonderfully creative in the kitchen. Variations can be almost endless."

—United Press International, December 15, 1985

"You must also put on really good music. And pour yourself a good glass of wine. A sauterne, maybe a chateau d'Yquem, 1983. And it's nice if your wife sits there and talks to you. It's a good time to hash over the party. For me, that is sometimes the nicest part of a party, if I had a good time."

—On how a husband should help his wife clean up after a dinner party, *London Guardian* (London, England), September 16, 1996

on decorating

"Edit. Decide what you really want in a room. Don't get cluttered."

—On choosing furniture, *Houston Chronicle* (Houston, Texas), May 24, 2003

"They feel softer than any baby's skin you've ever felt, any fabric. It's more beautiful than stone."

—On her line of paints, *Palm Beach Post*
(Palm Beach, Florida), February 4, 1996

"I want to be able to use every single thing myself in whatever home I happen to have."

—On her Kmart products, *Hamilton Spectator*
(Hamilton, Ontario, Canada), March 3, 1997

"You should use a number of different colors in each room."

—*Roanoke Times* (Roanoke, Virginia), February 21, 1997

"The colors for the paints come from everywhere—my eggs, my flowers, even my pets. We sat with my five cats and three dogs and looked through their fur for inspiration. One cat alone gave us 13 colors."

—*Albany Times Union* (Albany, New York), February 20, 1997

"The more the merrier."

—On "overdecorating" with Christmas lights, *Newsday*

(Long Island, New York), December 17, 2000

Bryant Gumbel: *With so many ornaments available, why would I want to spend so much time making ornaments?*

Martha Stewart: *Because homemade ornaments make a tree that looks like this fantastic craft-paper tree. There's not very many trees that look like that anymore. I mean, they get to be too gaudy; they get to be too ordinary. And I think handmade ornaments, year after year, if you add to your collection with homemade things, you can say, "Oh, I made that in—in the year 2000." People do that, Bryant. This is heirloom kind of stuff.*

—*The Early Show*, CBS, November 28, 2000

"It all starts with color for us."

—*Chattanooga Times Free Press* (Chattanooga, Tennessee), May 4, 2002

"The great thing about it [Turkey Hill furniture collection] is you're getting heirlooms of tomorrow today. These are pieces that can be usable for many years. . . . A chair might be $300, a giant armoire may be $2,000. In comparison to what is out there, this is better made."

—The News & Observer (Raleigh, North Carolina), October 18, 2003

"What we really wanted to do is create an easy way for America to put together a room or an entire house. We hope these pieces will become tomorrow's heirlooms. This is furniture that's not going to be out of date in a few years."

—On Martha Stewart Signature Furniture, *Miami Herald*

(Miami, Florida), May 3, 2003

on holidays

"If you mist your tree, then you can't mist your ornaments and you can't mist the electric lights. But you should water it if it's live. We've actually pruned branches, giving more space in between the branches to show off the ornaments that we're making."

—*The Early Show*, CBS, December 12, 2001

"Halloween night commands most of the elements of a first-rate party: good company, fancily or fancifully dressed; a charged atmosphere full of laughter and shadows; candlelight, and a rare stretch of free time, particularly for a school night."

—*Cambridge Reporter* (Cambridge, Ontario, Canada), October 24, 2001

"Those who have been keeping close watch over the children [on Halloween] will particularly appreciate being greeted with an Eyeball Highball—a martini served up with an all-seeing radish and olive ice cubes."

—*Edmonton Sun* (Edmonton, Alberta, Canada), October 24, 2001

"You can make a children's tree of rickrack ornaments. You start now, in a hundred years, you'll have enough."

—Poking fun at herself, *Star Tribune* (Minneapolis, Minnesota), November 15, 2003

"I get a little carried away at this time of year."

—*Dallas Morning News* (Dallas, Texas), December 12, 1995

"I don't want to be a preacher, but in the time it takes to do all that moaning and groaning, you can make a cranberry wreath."

—When people say they don't have enough time to decorate for the holidays,

USA Today, December 12, 1995

"I love the festivity of Christmas. Year after year I have tried to remember all the good and beautiful things about this most joyous of holidays."

—Business Wire, November 21, 1989

"I think we've had it with silly gifts. I believe in the kind of gift that will last forever."

—*USA Today,* November 3, 1989

"I really like keeping tradition alive and encouraging people to think about the holidays positively. I hate to see people so worried about not having enough money to buy presents because that's what sort of ruins Christmas. People overextend themselves at Christmas time when a homemade box of cookies would be just as nice as a diamond ring. Really and truly, I think that. It's more the tradition. It's more the thought than the expenditure. What I do is based on creativity, and a lot of it is very noncostly. Making paper ornaments. What can be cheaper? Making cookies. Cheap as can be. Wrapping presents with glassine, tissue paper and string. They are beautiful."

—*St. Petersburg Times* (St. Petersburg, Florida), December 10, 1996

"Well, they can certainly do less than 42,000."

—On what other people can do if they don't have the time or the money to copy a Christmas tree she decorated with 42,000 lights, *Vero Beach Press Journal* (Vero Beach, Florida), December 5, 1999

"These are our little gobblers. This sounds mean, but they really are delicious. They love the cold weather. Little do they know."

—On a huddle of cute and fuzzy little baby turkeys, *Press-Enterprise* (Riverside, California), November 12, 1995

"It was always a very big family meal full of the traditional food, with all our ethnic insertions—like hearty mushroom soup. Fresh fruit salad started the meal, and for dessert there were pies—always mincemeat, apple and pumpkin. It was quite festive. Those were the days of Sunday best dishes. My mother used Irish damask cloths and her real silver, and my father or I did the flowers."

—On her childhood Thanksgivings, *Chicago Tribune* (Chicago, Illinois), November 20, 1988

"People would rather spend time taking a walk than cooking [a Thanksgiving turkey] for 24 hours."

—*USA Today*, November 25, 1998

"On our Web site, 'Turkey 101,' everyone should access that recipe because it is, I think, the best. I'm going to be baking my turkey that way. It's covered with cheese cloth and always basted with a little bit of butter and white wine and the turkey drippings. It's great."

—On the best way to cook a Thanksgiving turkey, *CNN Street Sweep*,

CNN, November 2, 2000

on fashion

"When I was a stockbroker, I was outrageous. I wore hot pants. I was one of the few women on Wall Street. I thought the way of dressing there was just stupid. I had beautiful long legs. I wore brown velvet hot pants with brown stockings and high heels."

—*Fortune*, August 5, 1996

"I love brown; it matches my eyes and is a pleasant change from somber black."

—*People*, September 14, 1998

"Buttons are the fossils of the sartorial world, enduring long past the garments they were designed to hold together."

—*Times Colonist* (Victoria, British Columbia, Canada), January 29, 2000

on food

"Most sheet cakes are horrid."

—*New Haven Register* (New Haven, Connecticut), April 11, 1996

"I have already sent my cookie and cake decorating kits to his wife. Hopefully, she will have something decorated for us by New Year's."

—On sending cooking materials ahead of time to the wife of

American University Egyptologist Professor Kent Weeks in Cairo,

New York Times (New York, New York), December 24, 1996

"These are very special. And it's not that they're so special, because mom and grandmom have been making these layer cakes for many, many years. But we just always think we don't have time to make them. All you need are enough pans and some flour and some sugar and some other ingredients, and you can make the most delicious cakes."

—*CBS This Morning*, CBS, April 29, 1997

"Well, you know, it's not bad breath, it's garlic breath."

—*CBS This Morning*, CBS, March 11, 1997

"Bryant and I are friends. I don't have to cook for him."

—Asked whether she will cook *CBS This Morning* host Bryant Gumbel's favorite foods on the show, *Electronic Media*, February 10, 1997

"These products are utilitarian, practical, beautiful, classical and, above all, indispensable to all home cooks. They are must-have essentials in any kitchen anywhere, anytime."

—On her line of copper-bottomed pots, *Toronto Star* (Toronto, Ontario, Canada), November 26, 2000

"I've been drinking lattes, that's probably why I'm talking so fast. I'm jazzed up."

—Speaking to a crowd in Toronto about her new line of kitchenware, Canadian Press Newswire, November 19, 2000

"Nibble only when you've blown out the candle."

—On candy corn placed in a jelly jar with a votive candle on top for a Halloween decoration, *Boston Herald* (Boston, Massachusetts), October 25, 2000

"People slurp their noodles in Japan. They eat with their fingers in Iran. Still, politeness, a smile, and being nice are universal."

—*The Record* (Bergen County, New Jersey), April 25, 2000

"The dining room is a defunct room in the house these days. People eat in the kitchen."

—*Food Processing*, April 1, 2001

"To tell you the truth, I have not been able to chop a cabbage since . . . [the TV show where she tried, unsuccessfully, to sidestep questions about ImClone]. No more coleslaw for me."

—The Associated Press, November 6, 2003

"To go home and eat out of the can or standing at the refrigerator is not my kind of thing. It's nice to make a fluffy omelet. It's nice to go out and pick a salad from the garden and wash it and look at it and make something tasty. I think all of that helps you feel better, live longer and enjoy life more."

—*Vancouver Sun* (Vancouver, British Columbia, Canada),

September 11, 2003

"It's elliptical. It's everyday food, and food every day. I like that."

—On her Everyday Food products, *New York Times*

(New York, New York), June 26, 2003

"I was lucky. I started catering just when people were getting interested in food. I was organized and I had a knack for making things look good. And I had no problem cooking for large numbers because I came from a big family and was good at math. I just took my favorite recipes and multiplied them."

—*Newsday* (Long Island, New York), March 15, 1989

"People think because I haven't worked in a restaurant that I haven't paid my dues. I am not a chef, but I do my own cooking and my own creating. If you have an idea, you should make it your own idea, with your name, your face."

—*Time*, December 19, 1988

"The process of browning the meat gets the meat to be the right color so it's not an insipid gray when you finally get it to the table. You know how some stews come and they're kind of, 'Ew! My gosh, what did they do to that?' Well, they didn't brown it and they didn't deglaze it. That's for sure."

—*The Early Show*, CBS, October 17, 2001

on style

"It's not just home furnishings. It's the clothes you wear, the cars you drive, the foods you eat, the perfume you wear. The interest in high quality, good quality and lasting quality is what has spurred this tremendous interest in living. People want quality in their lives."

—*London Independent* (London, England), September 24, 1995

"Style is of the utmost importance to us."

—*Contra Costa Times* (San Francisco, California), October 21, 2000

"We are reliving living as an art form."

—*The Observer* (London, England), May 5, 1996

"I think some people just don't get it. They think that I'm telling everybody that they have to do this or they have to do that. I'm just showing people how things are done, hoping that someday it will be useful."

—*St. Petersburg Times* (St. Petersburg, Florida), December 10, 1996

"My writing is in a way that doesn't talk down to anybody. It's not unessential information. Even if it's a simple thing like how to fold a napkin or how to make a napkin ring, it's pretty essential even if you don't use it."

—*Orange County Register* (Orange County, California), January 27, 1996

"I still love beautiful linens and dishes and tableware and flowers. In my personal style, it's sort of just evolving. It changes. It's a little more casual."

—*Washington Post* (Washington, D.C.), December 19, 1998

"I have a pretty broad mind and good taste. Things I like other people will like."

—*Chicago Daily Herald* (Chicago, Illinois), March 22, 1998

"We don't want you to have clunky-looking stuff."

—*Washington Post* (Washington, D.C.), October 14, 2000

"To me, design is not fashion or faddism. Design is something one develops. I've been influenced by so much, mostly by what I've seen and what I've studied."

—*Chicago Tribune* (Chicago, Illinois), November 25, 2001

"Our products are affordable but still wonderfully designed and decorative. . . . We are bringing tradition back into the home, but we're not being fuddy-duddy at all."

—*Chattanooga Times Free Press* (Chattanooga, Tennessee), May 4, 2002

"What I try to do is bring back a way of life that we've forgotten. It began to change in the 1970s with the 'Me Generation.' But now we're looking for a balance with our career, homes, gardens, family and pets. I try to show a comfortable and gentle lifestyle from the moment you wake up until you go to bed in a very nice way that's not expensive and from a woman's way with the subject of life."

—*Albany Times Union* (Albany, New York), September 24, 1995

"In our educational way, we are making people realize that they do have a sense of aesthetic. That's why our appeal is so broad. It's for people with lots of money and not so much money. People don't want 15 suits. They want three good ones."

—*Los Angeles Times* (Los Angeles, California), June 17, 1995

"I see no division between the type of merchandise at a mass-market store and a department store. My table settings mix inexpensive things with my own family heirlooms and collectibles and things I get from the gardens and from nature."

—*Christian Science Monitor,* March 25, 1988

"With good posture, you will always look terrific. I take Polaroid pictures of them [friends] in their usual stance. When they see the photos, they straighten up."

—*People,* May 6, 1996

"But he did. And the entire photo shoot lasted only 30 minutes."

—On makeup artist Kevyn Aucoin's ability to transform her into

Veronica Lake in his celebrity makeover book, *Face Forward,*

New York Daily News (New York, New York), September 25, 2000

on weddings

"The cake defines the style of a wedding almost as much as a bride's dress."

—*The Best of Martha Stewart Living Weddings*, cited by Copley News Service, December 17, 2000

"Make it personal. You can't please everybody so you might as well please yourself."

—*Buffalo News* (Buffalo, New York), June 18, 1995

"Not much has changed in weddings. The traditional veil that covers the bride's face and is lifted at the end of the wedding ceremony still works. Hair should look polished. Brides should never have to wear tortured hairstyles on their wedding day."

—*Orange County Register* (Orange County, California), April 14, 1995

"They are showing up at the meal-planning session and really taking part. I got a letter once from a groom saying the menu we had planned wasn't quite right and could we think of something else, which I thought was great because he really wanted to have a say."

—On grooms participating in wedding plans,

Chicago Tribune (Chicago, Illinois), June 5, 1988

"See that you talk to two or three caterers before you make any plans, get very detailed estimates from each one, and then and only then, start planning. Take up offers of help. If a friend or relative wants to make the cake, accept and let them help with other parts of the reception too."

—*Toronto Star* (Toronto, Ontario, Canada), April 22, 1987

on her business
philosophy

"But because so many [companies] fail, MSL Omnimedia's strength and business sense stand out. We are a tortoise—going along at our own pace."

—*Regina Leader-Post* (Regina, Saskatchewan, Canada), November 20, 2000

"I'm the beech tree. I chose it because of how strong the beech tree is, how beautiful its skin is, and how impenetrable it is. Later I found out that the beech tree is the mother tree, so I realized this is very appropriate."

—On thinking of her company's managers as trees,

Fortune, October 12, 1998

"I really worked very hard to try to find a way so that I could really own my company and not give away any of it. We financed it internally."

—On Martha Stewart Living Omnimedia, *Mediaweek*, February 10, 1997

"Merchandising is going to be very important. Martha by Mail is destined to probably be one of our largest businesses."

—On her direct-mail unit that sells cooking and home products,

Advertising Age, February 10, 1997

"I think we have just begun to strike a nerve in America—the nerve that wants to learn and know and enjoy. There are a lot more people to reach. . . . We needed our independence to go forward."

—On buying back her company from Time Warner,

Philadelphia Inquirer (Philadelphia, Pennsylvania), February 6, 1997

"Time was a wonderful corporate parent, but it is basically a magazine and book publisher, not a television company or an online service or a merchandising company—and those are areas where I foresee tremendous growth for us."

—*Los Angeles Times* (Los Angeles, California), February 5, 1997

"If you love what you do and consider yourself a success, fine. But if you can't make money doing that, it is not a success. That's a lesson I learned from Wall Street."

—*Fairfield County Business Journal,* March 23, 1998

"It's not a premonition thing, it's totally evolutionary. One day you're one thing, the next you're something else."

—When asked if she knew how far her company could go,

Advertising Age, October 16, 2000

"It's an odd combination of business and creativity. We all have our fingers in the whole pie now."

—*New York Post* (New York, New York), September 22, 2000

"I don't want to be an evangelist, you know? I don't want to be. I think of myself more as a pilgrim, going out, discovering, setting roots, feeding, growing. The word I'm looking for is 'improve,' to think about themselves in a better way. You know, there's a lot of lack of self-confidence around . . ."

—*60 Minutes II*, CBS, June 20, 2000

"We've been very diligent in seeing that information and products reach as many people as possible."

—*HFN*, May 29, 2000

"We take that one idea and create a multiplier effect. We don't beat a dead horse, but we try to take a basic idea and extend it."

—*Post-Standard* (Syracuse, New York), March 24, 2000

"We don't take ourselves too seriously. An important part of business is to make fun of yourself because if you don't, someone else will."

—University Wire, March 15, 2001

"I'm always experimenting. I'm always continuing with my curious nature, always trying to discover new areas that have not been treated in a good way before. You know, we sort of made homekeeping a business. We made it a real business niche now. And so what's the next thing? I really think that maybe it is organizing the homemaker. I think that every one of us needs to be better organized. We want to have more time. We don't want to waste time. We want to make time for good things. We want to spend more time with our family. Look at you: two young kids. Don't you want to spend more time with the kids?"

—Larry *King Live*, CNN, February 2, 2001

"You can't disappoint even for a quarter. There's very little patience for failure."

—On running a public company, *The Record*
(Kitchener-Waterloo, Ontario, Canada), June 6, 2002

"It [the idea for your company] has to be great in one way or another. You have to have that vision if you're going to be a true entrepreneur."

—Canadian Press Newswire, June 4, 2002

"Always evolve, don't try to drastically change your business."

—*Providence Journal* (Providence, Rhode Island), April 26, 2002

"It was my original dream to be able to provide anyone with a really good product at really great prices—in a nice location."

—*The Halifax Daily News* (Halifax, Nova Scotia, Canada), September 9, 2003

"I left Wall Street, which was an extremely aggressive workplace and an extremely high-pressured place, to go home and to try to spend time with my daughter, fix up the house, paint the shutters and lay out the gardens, and it worked very well. I saw the value of that and turned it into a business."

—*Dateline NBC*, NBC, May 18, 2003

"We started out [in 1991] as a magazine for the homemaker. And now, because of our peculiar social system, we have become much more. The male segment of our audience is growing faster than [the] female. We've created what is considered a non-conventional, future-forward company."

—*New Haven Register* (New Haven, Connecticut), April 11, 1996

"We pioneered a new media category which is called lifestyle. Nobody else ever did it before, and we did it, and we intend to really dominate this area for a very long time to come."

—*Commercial Appeal* (Memphis, Tennessee), October 20, 1999

"The reason I want to spend so much money [on TV production] is because I'm compiling a library of correct procedures for gardening and home projects that can be available through computers in the information age."

—*Chicago Tribune* (Chicago, Illinois), April 18, 1998

"Most designers start at the top of the pyramid with the highest price points and merchandise. We started at the bottom, with the widest spread, and are going up the pyramid. It's easier."

—On the marketing strategy for her Kmart brand,

HFN, September 20, 1999

on branding

"It's weird when you wake up one day and realize you are a brand. You have to learn how to cope with that. You have to learn how to be the brand and be yourself. I try to be natural about it. There isn't much difference between the public Martha and the private one."

—*Advertising Age,* April 10, 2000

"I am a brand."

—*Gallup Management Journal,* November 6, 2000

"I think everyone wonders, 'What the heck are we making cookie cutters for?' You're not just buying a cookie cutter, you're buying a way to use a cookie cutter."

—*Brandweek,* March 4, 1996

"Why not take good messages to less fortunate people?"

—The Associated Press, July 29, 1998

"Martha Stewart the person built Martha Stewart the brand."

—*New York Times* (New York, New York), October 8, 1996

"My name is on everything and, because of that, I want to make sure I'm offering quality. This is not a case of slapping a Pierre Cardin logo on a toilet cleaner, like I've seen in Japan."

—*Toronto Sun* (Toronto, Ontario, Canada), June 4, 1998

"Tell them Martha sent you."

—On returning defective branded products to stores, *Calgary Herald* (Calgary,

Alberta, Canada), May 30, 1998

"I went to the ladies room there, and it was fine. If the team [that closed it] is going to be that tough, I'm not going to have any problems."

—On inspecting a restroom at a factory in Egypt that her team

said didn't reach their standards and was temporarily closed,

Toronto Star (Toronto, Ontario, Canada), May 30, 1998

"You have to readjust the zeros in your head. That has been the hardest thing."

—On selling millions of pillows and towels of the

Lilac Garden bedding pattern, *HFN*, March 16, 1998

"It's a very nice business because we're providing growers bunches of information on how to arrange and how to take care of flowers."

—On *www.marthasflowers.com*, *Providence Journal-Bulletin*

(Providence, Rhode Island), February 12, 2000

"We are very proud of our company. We really do the design of our products in-house. It's a vast job, but to be able to control in-house protects the brand. We do not license the name."

—The Associated Press, June 14, 2000

"I hope my brand will outlive me by centuries."

—*National Post* (Toronto, Ontario, Canada), November 16, 2001

"The emphasis is definitely on total home decorating, top to bottom. That integrated, comprehensive approach is vital to the specialty consumer, and will really allow us to grow the whole Signature segment."

—*HFN,* November 5, 2001

"We think that it is a viable idea. We have not gone out to sell it yet."

—On a branded after-school program for children, *National Post*

(Toronto, Ontario, Canada), June 20, 2002

"In no way has this brand been tainted. It would certainly appeal to other retailers."

—On how Kmart's financial problems would reflect on her brand,
New York Times (New York, New York), January 26, 2002

"It will sell if I'm alive or dead."

—On the power of her brand, *National Post*
(Toronto, Ontario, Canada), October 18, 2002

on the internet

"*What we are here for on the Internet is to save people time, to give people time for other things, to provide them with products when and where they want them so that they can get on with living. I really feel strongly about that.*"

—*Adweek*, November 12, 2001

"*I don't think there is a speck of downside in the Internet. I think that we are suffering some major glitches right now. A lot of my friends' companies are not doing very well or now don't exist any longer. But it was an experiment, a very, very vast experiment trying to make an instant business. And what you learn—and what I have been taught in running a business—is that there is no such thing as an instant business.*"

—*Larry King Live*, CNN, February 2, 2001

"Don't look up Martha Stewart on the Internet, you will get a lot of crap. Just don't go there."

—*Providence Journal* (Providence, Rhode Island), April 26, 2002

on kmart

"How else could I reach 77 million people?"

—*Los Angeles Times* (Los Angeles, California), April 15, 1997

"I'd like to be on the board someday."

—*San Diego Union-Tribune* (San Diego, California), May 14, 2000

"Our ultimate goal is to get everyone in America to go to Kmart."

—*DSN Retailing Today*, October 23, 2000

"The Kmart shopper trusts me more than her lawyer or even her doctor."

—*New York Times* (New York, New York), February 27, 1997

"Whether the people are shopping at Kmart because they don't have enough money, they are frugal or looking for value, they are the kind of people I want to reach."

—*Advertising Age*, February 24, 1997

"I'm making things that I want, and if I would want them, I think my friends will want them. I think that, with some education, the Kmart shopper will want them too. Everybody likes nice things, and the whole objective here is that there's good design and mediocre design, and I really want to bring good design to Kmart in as many products as I can."

—*Chicago Tribune* (Chicago, Illinois), October 1, 1989

"The average Martha shopping basket is more expensive than the average Kmart basket."

—*Contra Costa Times* (San Francisco, California), May 7, 2000

"If we're going to stay in Kmart in a huge way, there's no reason we wouldn't go into more departments."

—*Deseret News* (Salt Lake City, Utah), May 2, 2000

"The addition of live plants and seeds to the line enables consumers to choose from a unique selection previously unavailable to the mass market, and our tools and other garden accessories are extraordinarily well made and beautifully priced. We are going to change the way America gardens."

—*Seattle Times* (Seattle, Washington), March 11, 2000

"We want [the consumer] to be successful from day one."

—On the introduction of lawn and garden products,

National Home Center News, March 6, 2000

"Ineffectual and unimaginative [Kmart's management in 1987]. That's when the slide began. . . . With [Chairman Floyd] Hall [in 1997] we revitalized the entire program. That's the way it should have been all along."

—On consulting with Kmart the first time in the late 1980s and when

their relationship took off in the late 1990s, *Detroit Free Press*

(Detroit, Michigan), February 10, 2000

"They were very Midwest. This was Kmart. This was maroon and black and dark green. It was bad."

—On her first experience consulting with Kmart, *BusinessWeek*,

January 17, 2000

"We haven't even had time to think about apparel."

—On whether she considered creating a clothing line, *WWD*, June 22, 2001

"If you're frustrated, keep looking. They will be restocked."

—On her products running out, *Detroit Free Press*
(Detroit, Michigan), June 14, 2001

"We have a large portion of each of those departments, which would be unlikely with any other retailer."

—*CBS MarketWatch*, CBS, January 9, 2001

"If they do declare bankruptcy, it's up to them to tell us if they want us in the mix or not."

—*Newsweek*, January 28, 2001

"Hopefully, there are other opportunities if something bad happens to Kmart. But we've taken the position that we're not going to talk about those opportunities right now."

—*Chicago Tribune* (Chicago, Illinois), March 5, 2002

"We have been working with them [Kmart] for 15 years. It's pretty hard to run out on a partner that's down. You know, that's not our style."

—*CNN.com*, February 8, 2002

"I am trying to encourage the Kmart customer to be more luxurious."

—*Orange County Register* (Orange County, California), March 22, 1997

"We are trying to create the best that you can afford."

—The Associated Press, June 13, 2000

"This first line is very traditional. We're not high fashion. We don't want to be high fashion. That would be inappropriate for the every-day kitchen."

—*Detroit News* (Detroit, Michigan), October 4, 2000

"In merchandising, we experienced resounding success with our kitchen offerings as customer demand exceeded initial expectations for these high-quality products at reasonable price points."

—*HFN*, November 6, 2000

"I love the small stuff. I want to make sure that this spatula not only works really well, lasts forever, I want it also on the back saying 'not all stainless steel is the same. The stainless steel that this utensil is made from is classified at 18/8. It's the best stainless steel for this particular job.' We're educating the public."

—*Your World with Neil Cavuto*, Fox News Channel, October 3, 2000

on her magazine

"There is always room for another good thing."

—On competition from *O* magazine, *New York Times* (New York, New York), April 19, 2000

"There are eight to 10 pages in the edit well, it's amazingly beautifully illustrated [and] there are the glossaries, which we pretty much invented. That makes it stand apart."

—*WWD*, December 8, 2000

"We thought the television program might cannibalize the magazine. It had just the opposite effect. We got more subscribers to the magazine; we got more people to watch the program as a result."

—*Daily Yomiuri* (Tokyo, Japan), November 18, 2000

"It's about how to do things and not about how to buy things."

—*Houston Chronicle* (Houston, Texas), December 31, 2001

"There was nothing like it. It gave how-to information and beautifully photographed stories. The magazine has become very valuable to all demographics, from farmers to waitresses to college students."

—*Milwaukee Journal Sentinel* (Milwaukee, Wisconsin), October 28, 2001

"My favorite parts [of the magazine] are the flowers and the cakes."

—*New York Daily News* (New York, New York), April 14, 2005

© Corbis/Savino Tony/Corbis Sygma

on fame

"I like human-interest stories, and I like well-researched stories. I've been the subject of a lot of badly researched stories."

—*Editor & Publisher Magazine*, October 9, 2000

"Oh, great. I'm in real fine company."

—On being on the cover of *Newsweek* and learning from the magazine's editors that most of the people who make the cover are murderers, terrorists, sexual deviants, or dead, *New York Daily News* (New York, New York), December 7, 1998

"When I was a model—and I was all during high school and college—you always wanted to be on the cover of a magazine. That's how your success was judged—the more covers the better. Well, I am the CEO of a New York Stock Exchange–listed company and I don't want to be on any covers of any newspapers for a long, long time."

—Commenting on the ImClone situation,

The Associated Press, June 25, 2002

"Those traits and that behavior [driven and sometimes insensitive] if it were applied to a man, would be admirable. Applied to a woman, you know, she's a bitch."

—*Ottawa Citizen,* (Ottawa, Ontario, Canada), November 6, 2003

"I was bumped for a very sad and horrible reason. But you were totally right to change the cover."

—To Walter Isaacson, managing editor of *Time,* on hearing that her cover was bumped in place of Princess Diana, who had just died, *New York Daily News* (New York, New York), November 24, 1998

on home

"*Some people like to collect paintings or dogs. I collect houses. It's also because I can't sell any of them because it's just too painful.*"

—The Associated Press, October 15, 2003

"*We had no money. We found this place, because it didn't cost anything. Unfortunately, what we did right away was put heat in it. We shouldn't have. I was sorry I made any improvements.*"

—On the first house she bought after marriage, *Commercial Appeal* (Memphis, Tennessee), December 22, 1996

"It was a great challenge to figure out what to do with this three-room, travertine shoebox. I was told to call John Pawson; I met him and really, really liked what he does."

—On buying the Gordon Bunshaft house in East Hampton,

New York, *Newsweek*, October 28, 1996

"Basement smells BAD, look for cat poops, change litter. Happy Valentine's Day."

—Note to gardener Renaldo Abreu, *Miami Herald*

(Miami, Florida), October 3, 1996

"I haven't been able to sit down and enjoy my views for one minute since this legal harassment started."

—On her disagreement with neighbor Harry Macklowe over

view-blocking shrubs between their mansions in

East Hampton, New York, *Chicago Tribune*

(Chicago, Illinois), April 6, 1997

"It has a fan, so it's cool, and it's big. When you go in, you just sort of keel over from the smell of cedar."

—On rebuilding part of her attic into a cedar closet designed to repel moths, *New York Times* (New York, New York), April 12, 1998

"Guess what already happens at my house? I don't want people stomping around in their shoes. In East Hampton, everyone takes them off."

—On what happens when people enter her home, *USA Today*, February 12, 1998

"I have four [homes]. I know, I can't remember [sometimes] . . . the houses are my laboratories . . . and I'm just starting on a new laboratory right now: a real farm. I'm building a new American version of the farm with all kinds of modern amenities for me and the animals but with the charm I hope that will instill in others a lot of inspiration and a lot of good ideas. So I'm excited by it."

—*Canada AM*, CTV Television, December 26, 2000

"I don't want to be a single person in a big house on a street with lots of other underoccupied homes separated by stone walls and locked gates. I don't want to have to plan my free time around traffic tie-ups and extended commutes. I don't want to feel isolated—feel that I'm missing something—by being so far from what interests me in the city."

—On moving out of Westport, Connecticut, to New York City,

Milwaukee Journal Sentinel (Milwaukee, Wisconsin), May 7, 2000

"As hard as it will be to leave my Westport home, I no longer feel connected to the neighborhood, the neighbors or even the town."

—*St. John's Telegram* (St. John, Newfoundland, Canada), April 15, 2000

"I've gotten seven dinner invitations from neighbors."

—After announcing that she will leave her home in Westport, Connecticut, *Dallas Morning News* (Dallas, Texas), April 14, 2000

"To be happy in a room, I don't need much. I need a view, I need air, I need light and nothing extraneous. I don't need a footstool and I don't need those pictures on the wall—if there's a view."

—*Houston Chronicle* (Houston, Texas), December 15, 2001

"Home is where we live. It's where we do most of our thinking, eating and, also, practice most of our hobbies."

—*Baltimore Sun* (Baltimore, Maryland), October 7, 2001

"It's great what is happening to the Hamptons. It is much more diverse than it was only 10 years ago when I bought my house."

—*USA Today,* July 31, 2001

on marriage

"I maintain a fabulous house, I have my pets, I have my daughter, I have my friends. I entertain. I'm not a miserable old divorcée. My life did not change drastically by not being married."

—*Chicago Tribune* (Chicago, Illinois), February 15, 1996

"It [my marriage] was not a stage set. Maybe it was too much for my husband—maybe he couldn't stand it. But I tell you, underneath it all I bet he loved it, and I'll bet a lot of people would love it. After my divorce, I made a pact with myself not to criticize or judge anymore."

—*The Australian* (Australia), January 25, 1996

"I'm sorry that I haven't spoken to him—or he hasn't spoken to me—for all these years."

—On ex-husband Andrew Stewart, Cox News Service, August 28, 2000

"It's pretty funny hearing so many wealthy guys bragging about the size of their weeping copper beeches and taxus yews. My theory is it's about midlife crisis. I've noticed that when they glimpse a rare tree and a pretty girl at the same time, they often look a lot more excited about the tree."

—*Ottawa Citizen* (Ottawa, Ontario, Canada), October 24, 1996

on pets

"*I think animals really add something to a household. I can't imagine a house that's empty, quiet, without any animals. I just think animals are charming. . . . The animals are always bringing me joy and always bringing me happiness. And when they're ill, I worry a lot about them. . . . All my animals are extremely pampered. In fact, most of my friends say they would like to come back as one of my pets.*"

—*The Oprah Winfrey Show*, ABC, July 30, 2001

"I have had eight, now seven of Jo's [Jo Ubogy, a breeder of Himalayan cats] spectacular cats. They come in pairs. First came Teeny and Weeny [in 1987], then Mozart and Beethoven, then Vivaldi and Verdi, and most recently Bartok and Berlioz. Poor Beethoven ran off the property and was found dead one mile from home. However, the rest are beautiful, healthy and happy. I love them so much!"

—*New York Times* (New York, New York), February 24, 2002

"It's [home] a very important place to me. That's where I grew up—in my professional life. It's where I sleep almost every night because of my animals [three chow chows, seven Himalayan cats, 15 chinchillas and 27 canaries], plenty of creatures who rely on human contact."

—*Plain Dealer* (Cleveland, Ohio), September 23, 2001

"Don't you poop on my jacket."

—To Harry the macaw during the announcement of *Petkeeping with Marc Morrone*, a cross-promotional TV venture, *Television Week*, April 28, 2003

on family

"I remember the first day that I was put out there on the garden path.
We had this cobblestone path in our garden and it had weeds in it.
And he [father] said, 'Take out all the grass.' I think I was three.
So I sat out there all day, you know, and I became his pet because
of that."

—*People in the News*, CNN, May 4, 2002

"Alexis [daughter] is the closest person in the world to me. She is a val-
ued confidante and counselor to me."

—*Pittsburgh Post-Gazette* (Pittsburgh, Pennsylvania), October 21, 2003

"It's still a total mystery to me. I loved my husband. I noticed him growing away, but I didn't pay any attention to it. He said I was too much for him, that I was going too far too fast. What does that mean? If I should be punished for being too critical or too perfectionist, I've been punished."

—*People*, November 28, 1988

"They're [family and friends] used to my workaholic schedule. And my life is my work and my work is my life."

—*People in the News*, CNN, May 4, 2002

on household chores

"*I want to elevate the role of the homemaker to a higher level. Home-making shouldn't be a drudgery.*"

—*Daily Yomiuri* (Tokyo, Japan), November 18, 2000

"*Stacking the dishwasher is also an art form that eludes a lot of us for our entire lives.*"

—*Esquire*, September 1996

"*Most people don't know how to take care of their houses anymore. Mothers forgot to teach the new generation.*"

—*Boston Herald* (Boston, Massachusetts), January 21, 1995

"Get that stuff off the bookcases that doesn't belong there and give those books you'll never read to the library for a sale. Get rid of that faddish junk you never use in those kitchen drawers. And take out that rosebush you hate. It's simplify, simplify, simplify."

—*Tampa Tribune,* (Tampa, Florida), May 10, 1995

"If you get tired of cooking, you can go outside and—and grow a plant. If you get tired of growing a plant, you can go canoeing. If you get tired of canoeing, you can just make a curtain, you can make a bed, you can paint a table, whatever."

—*60 Minutes II,* CBS, November 23, 1999

"There's been this great disillusionment in the last 10 years that maybe the workplace isn't all that fascinating—and that maybe the home and the kids need some help. There's a backlash out there and I'm part of it. I've always worked in the home. I do all my best thinking and creative work at home. I'm really just a homebody."

—*Calgary Herald* (Calgary, Alberta, Canada), October 24, 1998

"This may seem backward to some, but it makes perfect sense. When you fold the sheet back, the finished edge, monogram or other decorative detail faces up."

—On why the top sheet should be facedown on the bed,
Rocky Mountain News (Denver, Colorado), May 1, 2000

"I don't always do all of my own ironing, even though I wish that I could. I love ironing."

—*Ventura County Star* (Ventura, California), March 8, 2005

on some pet peeves

"I'm bothered by things that hurt people, like smoking, like drinking in excess, like being mean. If people choose to paint their house a hideous color, that doesn't bother me. I won't tell them outright their choice is really bad. But I'll do that for smoking."

—*Chattanooga Free Press* (Chattanooga, Tennessee), October 23, 1996

"His whites, he has so many whites. Do you want to know what that does to me? Drives me crazy. What I want to do is, if there is a white we love, to offer that white. The consumer's gonna say, 'Well, if Martha thinks this is the best white, it must be the best white.'"

—On how many shades of white Ralph Lauren has in his paint collection, *Fort Lauderdale Sun-Sentinel* (Fort Lauderdale, Florida), July 5, 1996

"The new Fiesta ware is insipid. Why do you need lilac? It's not a primary color. There's no need to water down the original."

—*Chicago Tribune* (Chicago, Illinois), May 6, 1997

"I hate it when I go into somebody's property and see ugly green hoses. They don't have to stick out in the landscape. That's why mine are gray or olive green."

—*Augusta Chronicle* (Augusta, Georgia), March 9, 2000

on the stock market

"*Because it's so diverse, MSL Omnimedia is hard [for stock analysts] to follow. The market sucks.*"

—On being unable to garner media attention on her company's wide range of products, *Halifax Daily News* (Halifax, Nova Scotia, Canada), November 20, 2000

"*You're only as good as your last meal if you're a caterer, and you're only as good as your last quarterly earnings if you're chairman of a company that's listed on the New York Stock Exchange. It's all the same. It's all about performance, growth and profitability.*"

—*New York Daily News* (New York, New York), November 1, 1999

"While some on Wall Street voiced concern that the entire New York–based company is based on one person's success and reputation, the person is separate from the brand. The brand has long-term contracts, the brand has magazines, the brand has 400 employees supporting it, and I think that's really what Wall Street wanted to hear and be persuaded on."

—*New York Daily News* (New York, New York), October 20, 1999

"It feels great. It really shows that people aren't just happy with our products but the company as well."

—On the opening day of her initial stock offering for Martha Stewart Living Omnimedia when she was told that the stock soared from $18 at opening to $52 a share, *USA Today,* October 20, 1999

OCTOBER 1

on the imclone debacle

"I've always been at the right place at the right time. This time I wasn't."

—*Fortune*, June 23, 2003

Martha Stewart had to agree to address the issue of ImClone in order to appear on CBS's *Early Show*. At first she sidestepped the issue:

"Hi, well, if we're going to make salad. . . ."

She was asked again to comment:

"Well, as you understand, I'm involved in an investigation that has very serious implications. I'm not at liberty at this time to make any comments whatsoever. . . . I think this will all be resolved in the very near future and I will be exonerated of any ridiculousness."

Then it was back to business as usual:

"I want to focus on my salad, because that's why we're here."

—The Associated Press, June 25, 2002

"I had no insider information. My sale of ImClone stock was entirely proper and lawful."

—*Vancouver Sun* (Vancouver, British Columbia, Canada), June 25, 2002

"The stock price had dropped substantially, to below $60. Since the stock had fallen below $60, I sold my shares, as I had previously agreed to do with my broker."

—*The Independent* (London, England), June 20, 2002

"The media focus on ImClone has generated an enormous amount of misinformation and confusion. Many have speculated about what might have happened."

—*The Record* (Kitchener-Waterloo, Ontario, Canada), June 20, 2002

"I did not want the media attention currently surrounding me to distract from the important work of the NYSE and thus felt it was appropriate to resign."

—On resigning from the board of the New York Stock
Exchange, The Associated Press, October 4, 2002

"It has been a great honor and privilege to sit on the board [of the New York Stock Exchange], but the rigors of my own very busy and demanding corporate life require my full attention at the present time."

—*Austin American-Statesman* (Austin, Texas), October 4, 2002

"Who wouldn't be scared? Of course I'm scared. The last place I would ever want to go is prison. And I don't think I will be going to prison, though."

—*Seattle Post-Intelligencer* (Seattle, Washington), December 23, 2003

"You have no idea how much worry and sadness and grief it causes . . . having done nothing wrong allows you to do things about other things. But there's always the worry. I mean a trial's coming up."

—Agence France Presse, December 21, 2003

"I certainly don't belong in that category."

—On being compared with executives in the Enron and WorldCom scandals, The Associated Press, November 5, 2003

"For a creative person to be maligned like this is the worst thing that could happen. It takes away the joy."

—*USA Today*, September 2, 2003

"The search for creative ideas, I can certainly continue to play that part. I now have more time to contribute more ideas. Damage also was done in the last year and a half that has to be repaired, and that's my job too."

—On stepping down as CEO and becoming chief creative

officer of Martha Stewart Living Omnimedia,

Orlando Sentinel (Orlando, Florida), June 26, 2003

"I want you to know that I am innocent—and that I will fight to clear my name."

—Advertisement in *USA Today,* cited by *Sunday Herald*

(Glasgow, Scotland), June 8, 2003

"I love this company, its people, and everything it stands for and I am stepping aside as chairman and CEO because it is the right thing to do. This will enable the company to continue to build the confidence and love of its readers, viewers, customers and strategic partners, without the distraction of my personal legal issues."

—Public statement on stepping down as CEO of

Martha Stewart Living Omnimedia, *AFX.com*, June 5, 2003

"It's sort of the American way to go up and down the ladder, maybe several times in a lifetime. And I've had a real long up. . . . And now I've had a long way down."

—*The Gazette* (Montreal, Quebec, Canada), January 28, 2003

on serving time

"I really missed lemons."

—People, March 21, 2005

"Although my lawyers remain very confident in the strength of my appeal—and will continue to pursue it on my behalf—I have decided to serve my sentence now because I want to put this nightmare behind me and get on with my life as soon as possible."

—CBS MarketWatch, CBS, September 15, 2004

"I know I have a very tough five months ahead of me, but I understand, too, that I will get through those months knowing that I have the ability to return to my productive and normal life, my interesting work and future business opportunities."

—CNN.com, September 15, 2004

"I will be joining more than two million other souls who are serving time. I would like to be back as early in March as possible to plant a new spring garden."

—*Journal News* (Westchester County, New York), September 16, 2004

"I cannot bear any longer the prolonged suffering while I and my legal team await vindication. I must reclaim my good life. I must return to my good works."

—Cox News Service, September 15, 2004

"It's odd what becomes of immense importance when one realizes one's freedom is about to be curtailed. It is frightening and difficult to grasp those realizations."

—*Newsday* (Long Island, New York), September 16, 2004

"I am obviously distressed by the jury's verdict but I continue to take comfort in knowing that I have done nothing wrong and that I have the enduring support of my family and friends. I will appeal the verdict and continue to fight to clear my name. I believe in the fairness of the judicial system and remain confident that I will ultimately prevail."

—The Associated Press, March 5, 2004

"Perhaps all of you out there can continue to show your support [while I am in prison] by subscribing to our magazine, by buying our products, by encouraging our advertisers to come back in full force to our magazines."

—After hearing her sentence, *Newsday* (Long Island, New York), July 17, 2004

"Whatever I have to do in the next few months, I hope the months go by quickly. I am used to all kinds of hard work, as you know."

—*Chicago Sun-Times* (Chicago, Illinois), July 18, 2004

"The only way to reclaim my life and the quality of life for all those re-lated to me with certainty now is to serve my sentence—surrender to the authorities so that I can quickly return as soon as possible to the life and the work that I love."

—*Miami Herald* (Miami, Florida), September 25, 2004

Martha thought she might serve time near her home, but she was not assigned to that facility.

"I do hope that there will be room at the Danbury facility, which is the prison nearest my home and close enough so that my 90-year-old mother and others can visit me."

—The Associated Press, September 15, 2004

"As you would expect, the loss of freedom and the lack of privacy [in prison] are extremely difficult. Visits from my friends, family and colleagues—together with your goodwill and best wishes—will get me through this chapter in my life."

—*Guelph Mercury* (Guelph, Ontario, Canada), November 24, 2004

"I want you to know that I am well. I am safe, fit and healthy, and I am pleased to report that, contrary to rumors you might have heard, my daily interactions with the staff and fellow inmates here at Alderson are marked by fair treatment and mutual respect."

—The Associated Press, November 24, 2004

"I continue to be touched by the outpouring of support I have received from so many of you. I am also touched that supporters have sent . . . thousands of letters to me. I have been told that some of these letters have included gifts and money. Please know that while these gestures of friendship and support are deeply appreciated, any such items must be returned to the sender by prison officials. Instead, if you are so inclined, please make a donation to the American Cancer Society, a charitable organization that means a lot to me."

—*Charleston Daily Mail* (Charleston, West Virginia), October 22, 2004

"The camp is fine; it is pretty much what I anticipated. The best news—everyone is nice—both the officials and my fellow inmates—I have adjusted and am very busy. The camp is like an old-fashioned college campus—without the freedom, of course."

—The Associated Press, October 15, 2004

"There's something under here that I'm not going to show. Whoever is watching me knows exactly where I am."

—To a group of advertising executives on her court-ordered
ankle bracelet, The Associated Press, May 2, 2005

"I'm allowed to eat."

—Response when asked about dining in a restaurant during
her 48 hours away from house arrest for work,
United Press International, March 19, 2005

"The night before I left she handed me this and said, 'Wear it in good health.' I hope she is reading the news and looking at television because I'm so proud of her."

—On wearing a much-photographed poncho crocheted by
a fellow inmate, The Associated Press, March 8, 2005

"We're going to deepen our bond with the millions who read our publications and watch our television programs. We're going to engage and inspire new readers and new viewers for whom these topics may have seemed alien, unfamiliar or even—believe it or not—superficial."

—On getting back in touch with her customers,

Countdown, MSNBC, March 15, 2005

"It's not just mom, dad and the kids anymore. I've seen that and met these people."

—On seeing different kinds of families while in prison,

New York Daily News (New York, New York), March 8, 2005

"Starting now, we must communicate not only the 'how to' that we've been so proud of, but also the 'why' in our editorial content. Our passion is and always should be to make life better."

—On refocusing the company, *Newsday* (Long Island, New York),

March 8, 2005

"There's no doubt that the last three years have certainly been an adventure for me. Though stressful, I can say that I don't regret everything. I've had profound experiences, met extraordinary people, felt deeply loved by my family."

—On meeting with employees after her release, *Los Angeles Times*

(Los Angeles, California), March 8, 2005

"I love all of you from the bottom of my heart, and I'm really glad to be home."

—*Today*, NBC, March 8, 2005

"The judges, the lawyers, the prosecutors do not really know what it's like to be incarcerated. They do not know that time passes slowly, there are no good educational opportunities, there is little of value with which to pass the time."

—Letter from prison to newspaper reporter, *Saint Paul Pioneer Press*

(Saint Paul, Minnesota), March 8, 2005

"I tried to represent the values of dignity and grace that I cherish so deeply, even when it was really difficult. I hope I succeeded."

—*Live from . . .* , CNN, March 7, 2005

"I didn't really miss material things at all. It was kind of nice to have a rest from the material things."

—Associated Press Financial Wire, March 5, 2005

"Right now, as you can imagine, I am thrilled to be returning to my more familiar life. My heart is filled with joy at the prospect of the warm embraces of my family, friends and colleagues. Certainly, there is no place like home."

—*Guelph Mercury* (Guelph, Ontario, Canada), March 5, 2005

"The experience of the last five months in Alderson, West Virginia, has been life-altering and life-affirming. You can be sure that I will never forget the friends that I met here, all that they have done to help me over these five months, their children, and the stories they have told me."

—Agence France Presse, March 4, 2005

"Someday, I hope to have the chance to talk more about all that has happened, the extraordinary people I have met here and all that I have learned."

—The Associated Press, March 4, 2005

"I didn't miss the cappuccino. I missed the idea of cappuccino."

—*CNN.com,* March 4, 2005

"See what one can do with nothing?"

—Letter to Margaret Roach, editor-in-chief of *Martha Stewart Living,* detailing how she began a yoga class, crocheted, and used old molds to create a nativity scene for her mother, The Associated Press, March 3, 2005

"I have had time to think, time to write, time to exercise, time to not eat the bad food, and time to walk and contemplate the future."

—*Los Angeles Times* (Los Angeles, California), February 26, 2005

on her deal with sirius

"I don't know about you, but I was raised on the radio. I'm very excited about this. . . . Of all the things that I have done in the last few years with Martha Stewart Living Omnimedia, radio is actually one of the most enjoyable."

—Associated Press Financial Wire, April 19, 2005

"It has been our dream to bring our expertise in the lifestyle arena and our vast library of how-to ideas to radio programming. Just as we pioneered in the creation of the how-to lifestyle magazine and how-to television media categories, our new partnership with Sirius is breaking new ground in satellite radio."

—New York Times (New York, New York), April 19, 2005

on television and
her tv show

"We will pioneer a new type of morning television that is more community- and family-based and closer to home in its nature."

—On moving to *CBS This Morning*, *Baltimore Sun*

(Baltimore, Maryland), January 13, 1997

"I miss Katie and Matt already, but Jane, Mark and Jose are all very nice."

—On switching from NBC's *Today Show* to

CBS This Morning, *USA Today*, February 10, 1997

"It's my first day as an anchor. I'm getting mixed up."

—First time as guest host of *CBS This Morning*, *New York*

Post (New York, New York), November 24, 1998

"I am a serious journalist, despite what I have been reading about me. I have had a big interest in seeing how a people who are oppressed cope with daily living."

—On a trip to Havana as correspondent for *CBS This Morning*,

Miami Herald (Miami, Florida), January 16, 1998

"We're really hoping that it will be a nice alternative to the daytime programming that now exists."

—*Hamilton Spectator* (Hamilton, Ontario, Canada), August 28, 1996

"I'll be on every show. It may not be me rolling out the pastries all the time, but it will be my show and I'll be hosting it."

—*Advertising Age,* August 26, 1996

"I hope to offer an alternative, something worthwhile to viewers. I think TV is in a rut."

—*Daily Variety,* August 26, 1996

"[Doing a daily show] will enable me to do longer projects, more projects and have some more continuity. Refinishing a chair might be fun to do over a period of a week. Even croissants take more than a day to make because you need time to let the dough rise."

—*Electronic Media,* August 26, 1996

"As we've watched the changing face of daytime television, we think stations are now interested in venturing beyond the traditional genres and into something that's rich in information and content, yet offers the security of the family."

—*Hollywood Reporter,* August 26, 1996

"That's the beauty of what I do. There is an unlimited amount of material to cover. What is hard is to make that material interesting, whether it's in the way it's shot, the way it's presented or the way it's researched."

—*Electronic Media,* July 13, 1998

"I think that we built our credibility on the fact that I was in my own environment, so that's what we've tried to do here."

—On making the set of her TV show mimic her home,
The Record (Bergen County, New Jersey), May 16, 1998

"I don't want this place to feel like a TV production studio. The goal was to design a workplace that is pleasant and healthy to work in and that inspires the creative process. There are lots of windows with views of the private grounds. I've also strived to keep the building low-profile and home-like out of respect for the neighborhood and residential character of the street."

—On building her television studio in Westport, Connecticut,
Stuart News/Port St. Lucie News (Stuart, Florida), May 11, 1998

"I was praying for the pierogies."

—On winning an award for the best national television cooking segment about baking wedding cakes but hoping that a show about a traditional Polish treat would win,
Pittsburgh Post-Gazette (Pittsburgh, Pennsylvania), May 7, 1998

"Every neighborhood has a few little crackpots. And there's one around here."

—On getting flak from neighbors about the studio built in Westport,
Connecticut, *Albany Times Union* (Albany, New York), May 2, 1998

"I really admire people that do regular TV programs every single day and are able to do so in environments that are totally unfriendly. For me, this is the friendliest studio that exists anywhere."

—*Hartford Courant* (Hartford, Connecticut), May 1, 1998

"Our shows are so superior to the others. In the quality of material, the lighting and camera work—we usually use four cameras instead of one. There's tremendous preparation and planning. We'll start a segment one year and finish it the next year if we have to."

—*Boston Globe* (Boston, Massachusetts), April 2, 1998

"This surge of patriotism that has occurred since the [9/11] attack has been quite inspiring, and this is a very nice way for us to participate."

—About a segment that will show the proper way to display the American flag, The Associated Press, October 4, 2001

"And buy a new car, because I can never figure out how to change those darn clocks."

—Making fun of herself in an April Fool's segment from her television show, *The Record* (Kitchener-Waterloo, Ontario, Canada), April 1, 2002

"I'd written all these books, and I had an idea called 'the beautiful how-to series.' Beautiful soups and how to make them, beautiful houses and how to build them, beautiful children and how to raise them. I thought, what format could work for this immense amount of information? And the only thing I could think of was a television show allied with a magazine."

—*Brandweek,* March 4, 1996

"There is a hope on the part of Mark Burnett, my executive producer, that my sense of humor will come out a little bit more."

—The Associated Press, May 3, 2005

"You're going to see a new Martha most people have never seen before."

—BPI Entertainment News Wire, May 3, 2005

on other people

"I told him everything I knew [about my deal with Time Warner]. And of course he proceeded to make a deal for Madonna that was infinitely superior to my little deal."

—On dinner with high-profile music celebrity lawyer Allen Grubman,

Los Angeles Times (Los Angeles, California), November 22, 1998

"Mrs. Clinton. How does she do it? You think you have insurmountable problems?"

—*St. Louis Post-Dispatch* (St. Louis, Missouri), May 29, 1998

"She got her ideas from the great French chefs and cooks, and she made it clear to the masses how those techniques were accomplished. The first time I made croissants from her recipe, they came out perfect. They were unsurpassed. That gave her huge credibility in my mind."

—On Julia Child, *USA Today*, December 1, 2000

"I'm going through eye-exercise therapy. I'm supposed to sort of, like, rest them. Probably, I could repeat the vice president's speech quite closely."

—On whether or not she was nodding off at a Democratic dinner,

St. Louis Post-Dispatch (St. Louis, Missouri), March 20, 1998

"Maybe you should build a bridge."

—To her hosts after a long wait for the ferry from Toronto's

Island Airport to downtown, The Canadian Press, November 19, 2000

"Rosie had to guess who I was."

—On appearing on the Rosie O'Donnell Halloween show dressed as

a bird lady, *Washington Post* (Washington, D.C.), October 29, 2000

"He deals with the powerful, the super-rich, the notorious, the good, the evil—he weaves a tale and makes it exciting and more interesting than almost anybody."

—On author Dominick Dunne, *Bangor Daily News*

(Bangor, Maine), August 15, 2001

"I came because Bill [Gates] invited me. I wasn't even invited by Charles."

—On her supposed romantic relationship with Charles Simonyl,

Microsoft engineer-turned-billionaire at a Silicon Valley gala,

Austin American-Statesman (Austin, Texas), August 13, 2001

"They never thought I would accept."

—On accepting an unlikely invitation to be on NPR's *Car Talk* radio show, *New York Times* (New York, New York), March 12, 2001

what other people say about martha

"*Martha is a unique combination of the beauty of the orchid and the efficiency of a computer.*"

—Mort Zuckerman, chairman, *U.S. News & World Report*,
in *People*, May 6, 1996

"*She works like a dog. She had a dream and she was clear about it from the beginning. I think she wants to run her own business, and I can't blame her for that.*"

—Susan Wyland, former editor of *Martha Stewart Living* magazine,
Palm Beach Post (Palm Beach, Florida), April 11, 1996

"The cultural meaning of Martha Stewart's success lies deep in the success itself."

—Joan Didion in *New Yorker* magazine, cited by
Sunday Herald (Glasgow, Scotland), June 18, 2000

"There's a phenomenon here of people who do what she says. I can't think of a precedent for the response she gets."

—Gene DeWitt of DeWitt Media, a New York–based media-buying agency,
Hamilton Spectator (Hamilton, Ontario, Canada), April 21, 1997

"I don't know whether I hate or love Martha Stewart."

—Connie Dagnan, co-owner of an Arlington, Texas, gourmet shop, about
how customers clamor for the latest cooking utensil Stewart uses on her show, *Fort
Worth Star-Telegram* (Fort Worth, Texas), February 3, 1997

"Stewart is one of the best self-marketers in this business. She's amazing—she appeals to ordinary women as well as upscale types."

—Steve Cohn, editor, *Media Industry Newsletter, Success,* February 1997

"She represents a dream, an impossible one. . . . Dirt and chaos are absent from the Martha Stewart world. Organic carrots from the kitchen garden are magically clean and compost never rots or smells."

—Kyla Wazana, Stanford University professor and the editor of a planned anthology,

No Place Like Home: Cultural Anxiety, Nostalgia and

Martha Stewart Living, Agence France Presse, October 7, 1998

"When we first introduced the Martha Stewart Everyday brand, Martha was often asked why she partnered with us. Her response? 'Kmart has an amazing ability to reach people.' And she's right. Millions of people shop our stores every day."

—Andy Giancamilli, president and general merchandise manager of

Kmart, *HFN*, September 28, 1998

"Natural gas is a lifestyle choice. If you were going to pick anyone who epitomized a good lifestyle, it would be Martha Stewart."

—Geralyn Johnson, Yankee Energy System spokesperson on having

Martha on the cover of the company's annual report, which read,

"Martha Stewart warms up to natural gas," *Vero Beach Press*

Journal (Vero Beach, Florida), January 12, 1998

"I think Martha changed the rules completely. The license programs traditionally had been through department stores. Martha Stewart was really a groundbreaker in saying you can do this at a good price point. Her impact has been monstrous. She has changed the way the business is done and has saved Kmart in the process."

—Warren Shoulberg, editor, *HFN, Daily News of Los Angeles*

(Los Angeles, California), December 9, 2000

"The two people in most people's lives who make them stressed out about Thanksgiving are their mother and Martha Stewart. You see all these beautiful, clever handmade things. You can't open a magazine and not see something beautiful for the table. You need to take a deep breath and come back to what you're doing and what you can manage."

—Party planner Bryan Rafanelli of Rafanelli Events, *Boston Herald*

(Boston, Massachusetts), November 19, 2000

"Martha makes real women—good women, women who don't get paid or have personal assistants to be professional homemakers—feel pressured and insecure. She's the human embodiment of everything that's wrong with so-called women's magazines."

—Letter to the editor from reader Sandy Voss, *Detroit Free Press*

(Detroit, Michigan), September 22, 2000

"Even as a child, you could see the promise. If there was a project . . . Martha did it. She took over, and it all fell into place."

—Her mother, Martha Kostyra, *Vancouver Province*

(Vancouver, British Columbia, Canada), July 9, 2000

"I'm sorry that Ms. Stewart never knocked on my door. Since her property was gated and electronically sealed, I could not knock on her door to offer her an invitation."

—Westport, Connecticut, next-door neighbor Bunny Grossinger Kaltman,

Plain Dealer (Cleveland, Ohio), May 9, 2000

"She was really very nice to me whenever I saw her. As a matter of fact, I used to buy eggs from her."

—Westport, Connecticut, neighbor Isabel Gordon,

The Associated Press, May 7, 2000

"I think she does a fabulous job. I aspire to have pages [in my magazine] as beautiful as Martha's. But Martha and I are not in competition with each other, because Martha is the queen of external creations, which I am not. I am really more interested in getting them to look inside themselves and to try to excavate, pull back the layers of their lives, and then fix up their house."

—Oprah Winfrey, *New York Daily News* (New York, New York), April 19, 2000

"I think Martha Stewart has proven that each of the different genres— magazine, Internet, radio, newspaper, television and cable on television—all complement each other and feed off of each other. . . . Martha is someone who understands her audience and her brand better than almost anyone."

—Ed Wilson, president of CBS-affiliated syndicator Eyemark Entertainment, which

distributes *Martha Stewart Living, Realscreen,* January 1, 2000

"It's Anti-Martha Stewart."

—Patricia Heaton on the messy house she lives in with Ray Romano on *Everybody Loves Raymond*, *Entertainment Weekly*, November 23, 2001

"She stays in touch just to invite me to her parties and gatherings that she might have, get-togethers. I don't speak to her, but she'll always send an invite or a 'Happy Holidays' card. That hospitality thing is for real with her."

—Rapper Busta Rhymes, who appeared with Martha Stewart on stage during the 1997 Video Music Awards, The Associated Press, September 7, 2001

"It's the haute bourgeoisie who have a problem with her—they're jealous of her. For what? That she manages to do everything so perfectly, I suppose. But the masses love her. That's the key. I think maybe it's that she always seems so perfect, you see. I think sometimes it would be nice if she said, 'My friend Suzie showed me this, and here's how she did it.' It's always that, 'I have done it. . . . '"

—Julia Child, *St. John's Telegram* (St. John, Newfoundland, Canada), August 11, 2001

"She's a really nice lady to work with. She didn't want to decoupage the animals or anything."

—Dave Siddon, owner of Oregon wildlife rehabilitation center
Wildlife Images, where Martha Stewart filmed a segment for
her show, *Wichita Eagle* (Wichita, Kansas), July 2, 2001

"She was much more interested in strangling this profile of her over which she had no control. . . . It was only after researching this book that I found out that was the kind of thing she did all the time."

—Christopher Byron, author of *Martha, Inc.*, an unauthorized and
unflattering biography of Martha Stewart, *Long Beach
Press-Telegram* (Long Beach, California), April 12, 2002

"We are saddened to lose Martha Stewart, who has built a brand and a company admired around the world. Our board will miss Ms. Stewart's counsel and insight."

—Dick Grasso, chairman and chief executive of the New York Stock Exchange, on Martha Stewart's resignation from the board of directors in the shadow of the ImClone investigation, The Associated Press, October 3, 2002

"Martha Stewart is being prosecuted not because of who she is but because of what she did."

—U.S. Attorney James Comey, The Associated Press, June 5, 2003

"It is pretty clear that people who come under government investigation panic, and sometimes the panic causes them to get into more trouble than what the government was looking at in the first place."

—Former federal prosecutor Lawrence Barcella, *Los Angeles Times* (Los Angeles, California), March 6, 2004

"I've always been fascinated by Martha Stewart. She has great style, great substance and she is actually very, very funny."

—TV producer Mark Burnett, *CNNMoney.com*, December 8, 2004

"She made a mistake. But she went in, she served her time, and she comes out hotter than ever before. I think she's bigger than ever before. She's got star power. She's got a magic to her."

—Donald Trump, Agence France Presse, March 6, 2005

"Martha is the little girl who sat in front of me in second grade. She never had mud on her shoes; I had to help put in the cows that broke the fence before school. On the day that I brought bittersweet to the teacher clutched in one grubby fist, she brought homemade candy decorated with candy roses in a box lined with paper doilies."

—An anonymous gardener, *Washington Post* (Washington, D.C.), October 29, 1995

"I don't know why people are so mean about her. Probably because she's so successful."

—Julia Child, *People*, October 2, 1995

"Everybody wishes they could duplicate her Connecticut style, it's her whole life they want to jump into. They want to have heirloom antiques like she does and have the guts to use them as tablecloths."

—Susan Friedland, senior editor, Harper & Row Publishers,
Washington Post (Washington, D.C.), November 30, 1988

"I would love to invest in her. She has a dazzling future going forward. She has no competitor."

—Mort Zuckerman, chairman, *U.S. News & World Report*,
Palm Beach Post (Palm Beach, Florida), April 11, 1996

"There's a great deal of status uncertainty out there, and it vibrates powerfully to the influence of someone who can assure you that you are doing the right, the tasteful, the elegant thing."

—Christopher Hitchens, journalist,

The Australian (Australia), January 25, 1996

"Martha is not tolerant of my negligence or my foolishness or my eccentricities. . . . We were too involved in our professional lives and in fixing up the house. We were always making the home a mythological place. But it wasn't a home."

—Ex-husband Andrew Stewart, *Sunday Times* (London, England),

January 21, 1996

"She's proven that a brand can begin with an individual and evolve into a total lifestyle."

—Kenneth Love, president, Lippincott & Margulies,

Investor's Business Daily, December 13, 1999

"Perfectionism is her greatest strength and greatest weakness."

—Martha's daughter, Alexis Stewart, *People,* December 13, 1999

"Unbelievable."

—Aretha Franklin on what it feels like to be in the kitchen with
Martha on her Christmas special, *Baltimore Sun*
(Baltimore, Maryland), December 8, 1999

*"Due to dangerous conditions, Martha Stewart has called off plans to
watch the millennium's first sunrise on top of a mountain. Instead,
Stewart said she'll make her own sunrise out of orange rinds."*

—Conan O'Brien on *Late Night with Conan O'Brien,* NBC,
cited by *Arkansas-Democrat Gazette*
(Little Rock, Arkansas), December 12, 1999

"People understand and need domestic fantasy. Martha Stewart author-izes them to dream."

—Mary Corbin Sies, a professor of American studies at the University of Maryland at College Park, *Chronicle of Higher Education*, November 19, 1999

"She picked them up like a lady and very delicately started to eat—very delicately, very sexually—she knows how to eat ribs. You know, I'm telling you, she makes it look very sexy."

—Ollie Gates, owner Gates BBQ, *Kansas City Star* (Kansas and Missouri), June 14, 1999

"She has an eroding self-esteem effect on American women. Martha is extremely exacting. If you actually try to plug in how she lives into your own life, you can be fraught with frustrations."

—Christopher Lowell, host of *Interior Motives*, *Pittsburgh Post-Gazette* (Pittsburgh, Pennsylvania), May 17, 1999

"Martha doesn't stop working but maybe for, I think she says, like, three or four hours a night, and then she's thinking about it while she's sleeping."

—Steve Ryman, merchandise vice president for the Martha Stewart Everyday brand
for Kmart, *Buffalo News* (Buffalo, New York), April 25, 1999

"What she's doing is appealing to the very high end and people who have a great deal of time on their hands."

—Lynette Jennings, who hosts a one-hour decorating and crafts show
five days a week, *Calgary Herald* (Calgary, Alberta, Canada),
March 6, 1999

"I am on your side. Because of you I have organized all the warranties and manuals in my house. Because of you I have a lovely dish soap in a cute bottle with a bar cap."

—Supportive fan Cynthia McKee of Lakewood, California,
on the *marthatalks.com* Web site, *Guelph Mercury*
(Guelph, Ontario, Canada), June 10, 2003

About the Editor

Bill Adler is the editor of four *New York Times* bestselling books, including *The Kennedy Wit* and *The Uncommon Wisdom of Jacqueline Kennedy Onassis*. He is also the president of Bill Adler Books, Inc., a New York literary agency whose clients have included Mike Wallace, Dan Rather, President George W. Bush, Bob Dole, Larry King, and Nancy Reagan.